Helpful Hints

Here are a few simple tips that will help with making beaded jewelry.

• These projects can be completed even if you are a beginning beader.

• Occasionally a wire will break or be too short - simply twist in a new piece of wire then continue beading.

• You don't have to follow any pattern exactly. Add your own personality with your favorite colors or different beads.

• The "vine pattern" necklaces are intended as guides. Follow the pattern as a basic guide, but feel free to mix and match beads, adding leaves, petals and buds in a random manner.

• With "vine pattern" necklaces, you often begin with 3 or 4 wires. Alternate adding beads on different wires so the wires will end up the same length.

• Loosely braid finished necklace wires together after you add all the beads for leaves, petals and buds.

• Twist wires together to form a small stem. This will hold beads and secure a leaf, petal or bud loop in place.

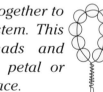

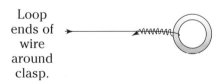

Loop ends of wire around clasp.

Twist ends securely.

Add a clasp to each end of a necklace by looping and twisting the ends of wires securely. Cut off excess wire.

Butterfly Necklace
pages 4 - 5

Flowers Necklace
page 6

Crystal Flowers
page 7

Sunny Brooch
page 8

Crystals Necklace
page 9

Buds Necklace
page 10

Tiny Flowers
page 11

Leaves and Buds
pages 12 - 13

Beautiful Brooch
page 14

Twined Vine
page 15

Fabulous Flowers
pages 16 - 17

Roses and Vines
pages 18 - 19

Beautiful Butterfly

Soft shades of blue bring a touch of early morning sky to this necklace.

An assortment of beautiful seed beads and crystals brings this dainty butterfly to life.

SIZE: 16" including clasp

MATERIALS: 11° seed beads (Blue, Medium Blue) • Twenty four 3mm Medium Blue crystals • Twelve 4mm Blue crystals • Seventeen 5mm Dark Blue crystals • Five 6mm Pale Blue bicones • Two 3mm Pale Blue crystals • 3/8" metal base • Clasp • 26 gauge Silver wire • Flat-nose Pliers • Wire cutters • E6000 adhesive

Twist wires together to hold beads and secure the tiny flower shapes in place.

How to Make a Butterfly

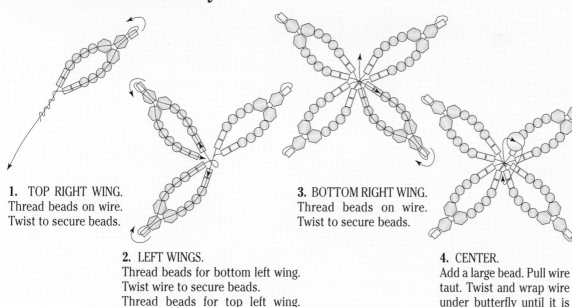

1. TOP RIGHT WING.
Thread beads on wire.
Twist to secure beads.

2. LEFT WINGS.
Thread beads for bottom left wing.
Twist wire to secure beads.
Thread beads for top left wing.
Twist wire to secure beads.

3. BOTTOM RIGHT WING.
Thread beads on wire.
Twist to secure beads.

4. CENTER.
Add a large bead. Pull wire taut. Twist and wrap wire under butterfly until it is secure. Set aside.

5. ANTENNAE.
Thread 2mm crystals on 3" long wires.
Twist each one to secure beads.
Make 2.
Set aside.

How to Make Necklace

6. Attach a 60" wire to each side of jewelry base.
Fold wires in half then twist each side about 5 twists to secure it.

7. Using 2 wires on one side of the jewelry base, thread on 9 beads. Twist into a tiny flower with a short stem. Twist for about 5 twists.
Add a crystal to one wire. Twist for about 5 twists.
Repeat to add more tiny flowers and crystals to desired length.

8. For the last 5", add bicone beads and twist for about 5 twists between each one.

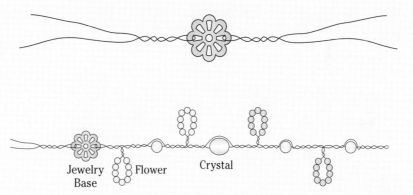

Jewelry Base   Flower   Crystal

9. Repeat beading pattern in a random manner on the other end of the necklace.
TIP: Alternate adding beads on different wires.
Add a clasp to each end of the necklace.

Continue Beading

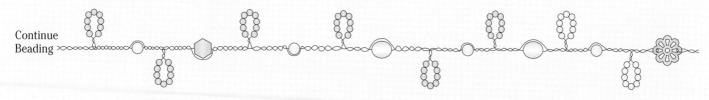

Finish the Necklace

10. Glue the butterfly to jewelry base.

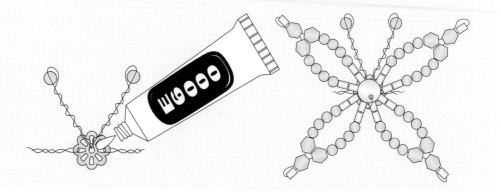

Small Flowers

Create this simple necklace in an evening.
Use delicate crystal beads for the beautiful
flowers and seed beads for the leaves.

SIZE: 16" including clasp
MATERIALS: Fourteen 5mm Green faceted crystals • 36 Green
3mm pearls • 11° Light Green seed beads • Clasp • 26 gauge
Silver wire • Flat-nose pliers • Wire cutters

1. Begin with 2 wires, each 48" long. Twist the wire together in
the center for about 1/2". Work out to one end, then work out to
the other end (this makes it easier to thread beads onto the
wire).

2. Thread 9 seed beads onto one wire. Form a loop.

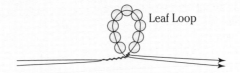

Leaf Loop

3. Twist wires to hold beads and form a short stem.
Twist the long wires together for 4 twists.

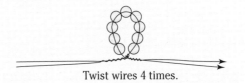

Twist wires 4 times.

4. Repeat to make a second leaf. Twist the wires together.
Make a flower and twist the long wires together.
Make 2 leaves and twist wires together.
Repeat this pattern to the end of the necklace.
Add a clasp to each end.

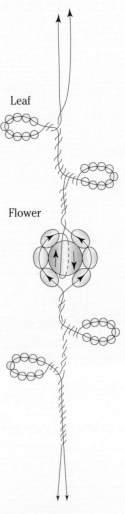

Leaf

Flower

The necklace pattern
has 6 flowers.

1. Begin with 2 wires, each 48" long. Twist the wire together in the center for about 1/2". Work out to one end, then work out to the other end (this makes it easier to thread beads onto the wire).

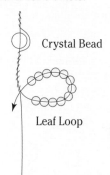

2. Thread a crystal bead onto one of the wires. Twist both wires together to secure the bead in place.

Thread on 12 seed beads. Form a loop in the wire for a leaf shape, and twist the wires to secure the loop and form a short stem.

Cross the wires and twist together for 5 twists.

Crystal Bead

Leaf Loop

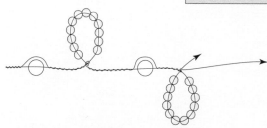

3. Thread on crystals for flower beads (see diagram below). Twist wires together to secure the beads.

Add one loop for a leaf. Twist to secure.

Add one small crystal spacer bead and twist to secure.

Add another loop for a leaf and twist to secure.

Repeat this beading pattern until you have 5 flowers (be sure to alternate the flower colors).

Add a clasp to each end.

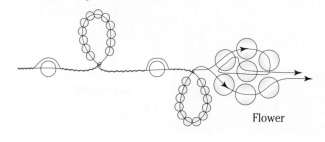

Flower

Crystal Flowers

Encircle your neck with the soft petals of pink and apricot roses when you make this feminine accessory.

This necklace is made similar to the Small Flowers Necklace on page 6 but with an added crystal bead as a spacer.

SIZE: 17" including clasp

MATERIALS: 7 mm faceted crystals (20 Apricot, 25 Light Green) • 3mm faceted crystals (8 Light Green) • 11° seed beads (Apricot, Light Green) • 28 gauge Green wire • Clasp • Flat-nose pliers • Wire cutters

Note:
Alternate the bead colors of the flowers.

Crystals Necklace

SIZE: 18" including clasp

MATERIALS: 8° hex seed beads (Pearly White and Clear) • Green beads (11° seed beads, 8° seed beads, E-beads) • Three 6mm Green crystals • 1/2" Green leaf beads • 30 gauge Silver wire • 26 gauge Green wire • Flat-nose pliers • Wire cutters • Three 1/2" leather circles • E6000 adhesive

FLOWERS

7. Make 12 Pearly White petals, 20 Clear petals and 3 stamens.

SIDE FLOWERS: Assemble 1 stamen and 4 Pearly White petals then twist wires together securely.

Add 5 Clear petals then twist wires together securely again. Twist tighter.

CENTER FLOWER: Make flower like side flower, then add 5 more Clear petals. Twist wires together securely again. Twist tighter.

8. Use Flat-nose pliers to twist wires tighter, then form wires into a spiral in back of the flower. Cut off excess wire.

9. Sandwich necklace wires between the flower and a leather circle.

Glue in place.

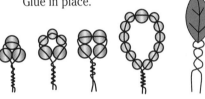

ASSORTED LEAVES
Add these on the necklace wires

Begin with 3 bugle beads

SMALL FLOWER PETAL
Make 12 with Pearly White beads

STAMEN
Make 3 with
Green crystals

LARGE FLOWER PETAL
Make 20 with Clear beads

Sunny Brooch

Add a touch of sparkle to your accessory wardrobe with this beautiful brooch.

Stamens
Make 8

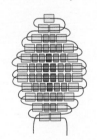

Petal
Make 12 Yellow

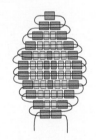

Leaf
Make 3 Green

Begin with 3
bugle beads

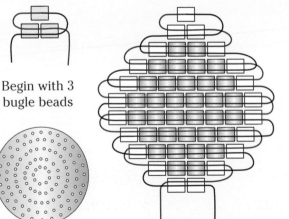

Metal Base

Petal / Leaf

SIZE: 4" diameter

MATERIALS: #2 bugle beads (Matte Yellow, Green, Red) • 11° seed beads (Orange, Red, Light Green, Green) • Eight 6mm Red crystals • 30 gauge Brass wire • Brooch base (1" perforated metal or a 1" octagon of 14 count plastic canvas) • 1" circle of leather • Pin back • Flat-nose pliers • Wire cutters • E6000 adhesive

1. Make 12 Yellow petals and 4 Green leaves.
2. Make 8 stamens (from Red bugle beads, seed beads and crystals) by threading wire up and down through the base.
3. Thread petal and leaf wires through to the back of the base (in 3 rows with leaves on the outside.
4. Twist wires on the back.
5. Trim excess wire and flatten all twists.
6. Glue a leather circle and pin to the back.

NECKLACE

1. Begin with 3 wires, each 48" long. Twist the wires together in the center for about 1/2".
2. Work out to one end, then work out to the other end (this makes it easier to thread beads onto the wire).

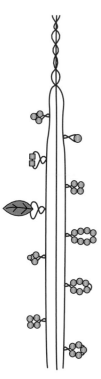

3. Add a set of beads to form a leaf. Twist the wire to secure the leaf with a short stem.
4. Add a set of beads to form another leaf. Twist the wire.
   Repeat beading pattern in a random manner to add leaves on the necklace.
   Alternate adding beads on different wires.
5. Loosely braid the wires together.
6. Add a clasp to each end of the necklace.

Crystals Necklace

Add sparkle to everything you wear. The basic colors of this beautiful crystal flowers necklace add glitter and beauty to every ensemble. Or choose your own brilliant colors for the fabulous flowers.

Simple Necklace

This simple necklace will complement your silk blouse, favorite dress or a pretty T-shirt.

Make it this afternoon, wear it tonight!

SIZE: 16" including clasp

MATERIALS: Pink beads (6mm faceted crystals, 4mm clear crystals, 4mm milky crystals, 4mm iridescent crystals, 3mm pearls) • Clasp • 26 gauge Pink wire • Flat-nose pliers • Wire cutters

Begin:

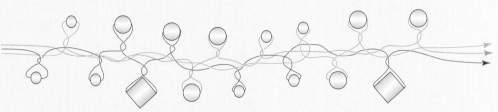

1. Start with 3 wires, each 36" long.

2. Twist wires together on one end.

3. String a bead or a group of beads and twist to form a short stem.

Repeat beading pattern in a random manner to the end. Alternate adding beads on different wires. Loosely braid wires together.

Add a clasp to each end.

Tiny Flowers Necklace

Entwine tiny flowers in an eye-catching necklace.

SIZE: 17" including clasp

MATERIALS: 3 blue dagger beads • 11° seed beads (Pink, Lavender, Aqua, Blue) • #2 Blue bugle beads • Twelve 3mm Pale Blue beads • 26 gauge Dark Blue wire • Clasp • Flat-nose pliers • Wire cutters

Twist wires together to hold beads and secure the tiny flower shapes in place.

Begin:

1. Start with one wire. Thread on bugle beads and an occasional dagger bead to desired length.

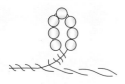

Bugle Beads   Dagger Bead

2. Begin with 2 wires, each 48" long. Twist wires together for 1/2" in the center.

3. Thread on 6 to 9 beads.

Twist into a tiny flower forming a short stem. Twist the 2 wires together for 5 twists.

Repeat to add more tiny flowers to desired length.

4. Intertwine the 2 beaded strands and the bugle beads strand together.

At the end, twist wires and add round beads to desired length.

Add a clasp to each end.

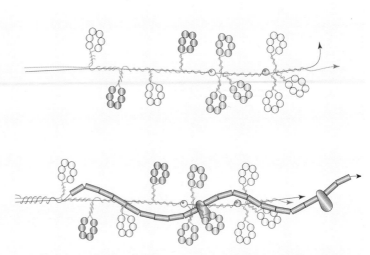

Leaves and Buds Necklace

Reminiscent of sunlight shimmering through the trees on a spring day, this necklace of leaves and beautiful pink buds is a one-of-a-kind creation.

SIZE: 16" including clasp

MATERIALS: 8 Green 15mm leaf beads • 2 Pink 15mm flower beads • Nine 5mm Clear Crystals • Twenty-three 3mm Pink Crystals • 11° Light Pink seed beads • 28 gauge Silver wire • Clasp • Flat-nose pliers • Wire cutters

1. Begin with 2 wires, each 48" long. Twist them together about 12" from one end.

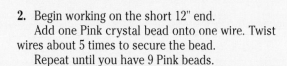

2. Begin working on the short 12" end.

Add one Pink crystal bead onto one wire. Twist wires about 5 times to secure the bead.

Repeat until you have 9 Pink beads.

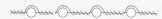

3. Now work on the longer end.

Add one leaf bead. Twist the wire to secure the leaf bead with a short stem.

Twist wires together about 5 times.

4. Add another leaf bead. Twist the wire to secure the second leaf bead with a short stem.

Twist wires together about 5 times and continue.

5. Add a Pink crystal and twist to secure.

SIDE FLOWER BUDS: Add Bud 1 (follow the diagram to add a Clear crystal with a seed bead on the end, then add two seed bead buds) twisting each section securely as you go.

Add Bud 2 (follow the diagram) twisting as you go.

Add Bud 3 (follow the diagram) twisting as you go.

6. Twist wires together as you return to the necklace.

Add a Pink crystal and twist to secure.

Add one leaf bead. Twist the wire to secure the leaf bead. Add a second leaf bead. Twist wire to secure.

Twist wires together about 5 times.

Add a Pink crystal and twist wires to secure.

7. CENTER FLOWERS: Add a bud (follow the diagram to add a Clear crystal with a seed bead on the end, then add two seed bead buds) twisting each section securely as you go.

Add Flower 1 (see diagram) twisting as you go.

Add Flower 2 (see diagram) twisting as you go.

8. Repeat SIDE FLOWER BUDS on the other side of the center flowers. Continue adding beads to make the necklace design symmetrical.

Add a clasp to each end of the necklace.

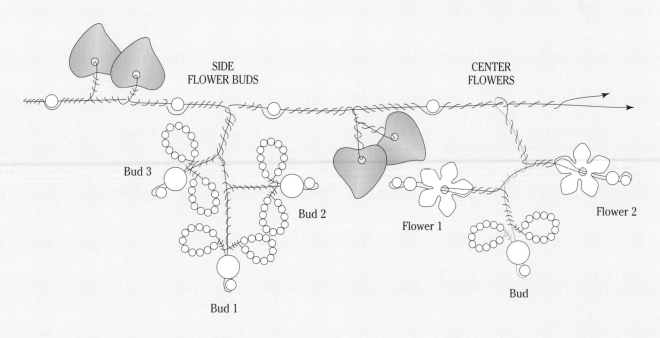

SIDE FLOWER BUDS

CENTER FLOWERS

Bud 3

Bud 2

Bud 1

Flower 1

Flower 2

Bud

Beautiful Brooch

All that glitters is not gold. This stunning brooch gets its sparkle from crystal clear and matte black beads.

SIZE: 2" diameter

MATERIALS: 11° hex seed beads (Clear, Matte Black) • #2 Black bugle beads • Seven 5mm Coral beads • Base (1" perforated metal circle or a 1" octagon of 14 count plastic canvas) • 30 gauge Silver wire • Flat-nose Pliers • Wire cutters • 1" leather circle • Pin Back • E6000 adhesive

ASSEMBLE FLOWER

1. Make 4 SMALL PETALS and 9 LARGE PETALS.
2. Make 7 STAMENS (from Coral beads, Black seed beads and Black bugle beads) by threading wire up and down through the base.
3. Thread petal wires from the front through to the back of the base.

Make 3 rows with 4 small petals on the inside, then 4 large petals on the next row, and finally 5 large petals on the outside.

Twist the wires to secure the petals in place.
4. Trim excess wire and flatten all twists.
5. Glue a leather circle and pin to the back.

SMALL PETAL - MAKE 4

Row 1A - 8 beads.

Row 1B

Row 2 - 8 beads.

Row 3 - 10 beads.

Continue beading rows: Row 4 - 12 beads, Row 5 - 11 beads, Row 6 - 9 beads, Row 7 - 7 beads, Row 8 - 5 beads.

Row 9 - 3 beads. Petal is finished.

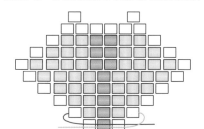

LARGE PETAL - MAKE 9

Row 1A - 14 beads.

Row 1B

Row 2 - 12 beads.

Row 3 - 14 beads.

Row 4 - 15 beads.

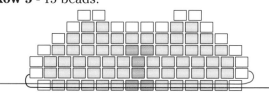

Row 5 - 15 beads.

Continue beading rows: Row 6 - 14 beads, Row 7 - 13 beads, Row 8 - 10 beads, Row 9 - 9 beads, Row 10 - 6 beads, Row 11 - 3 beads.

Row 12 - 2 beads. Petal is finished.

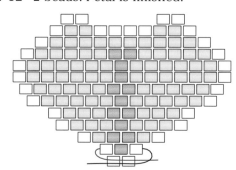

FLOWER STAMEN - MAKE 7

Stamen

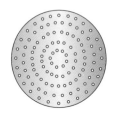

Metal Base

Make 7 STAMENS (from Coral beads, Black seed beads and Black bugle beads) by threading wire up and down through the base.

Twined Vine

Delicate blossoms shimmer in the sunlight with sunny beads. Sparkling leaves accent the bright flowers.

SIZE: 17" including clasp

MATERIALS: Five ³/₄" flat flower beads • Nine ¹/₂" leaf beads • 11° Green hex beads • 8° Pink seed beads • Pink E-beads • Clasp • 26 gauge Green wire • Flat-nose pliers • Wire cutters

1. Begin with 2 wires, each 48" long. Twist them together about 12" from one end.

2. Begin on the short 12" end.

Add one Pink seed bead. Twist wires about ³/₄" to secure the bead.

Repeat until you have 4 Pink beads.

Note: This diagram shows the necklace back view so you can see twisting the wire better.

Continued

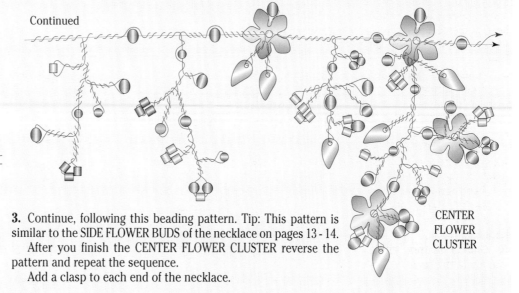

CENTER FLOWER CLUSTER

3. Continue, following this beading pattern. Tip: This pattern is similar to the SIDE FLOWER BUDS of the necklace on pages 13 - 14.

After you finish the CENTER FLOWER CLUSTER reverse the pattern and repeat the sequence.

Add a clasp to each end of the necklace.

SIZE: 19" including clasp

MATERIALS: Silver lined 11° seed beads (Orange, Purple, Red, Turquoise, Blue, Gold, Dark Green) • Nine 9mm Light Green crystals • Seven 6mm Red crystals • Eight Green leaf beads • 28 gauge wire (Purple for green, blue, turquoise, purple flowers, Copper for Red, Orange, Gold flowers, Dark Green for the stems) • Clasp •Flat-nose pliers • Wire cutters

How to Make a Flower:

Make 7 flowers.

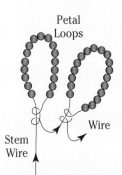

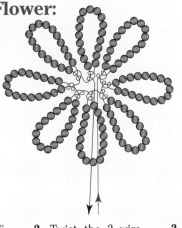

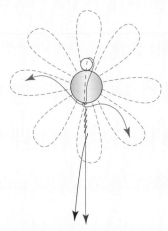

1. Thread 17 beads on 15" of wire. Form a petal loop with wire. Twist until secure.

Repeat until you have 8 petal loops.

2. Twist the 2 wire ends together to secure the petals in a circle.

3. Make a flower stamen for each flower with a Red crystal and a seed bead.

Twist wires together.

4. Place a stamen in the center of petal circle.

Position wires over opposite sides of flower and twist stamen ends together at the back.

How to Make the Necklace:

5. Begin with 4 wires, each 48" long. Twist the wires together in the center for about 1/2". Work out to one end, then work out to the other end (this makes it easier to thread beads onto the wire).

6. This diagram shows one section of the necklace. Use the same beading pattern for each section, just change the bead styles and colors.

String a bead or a group of beads and twist. Repeat beading pattern in a random manner to the end. Alternate adding beads on different wires.

Loosely braid wires together.

Attach Flowers

To attach flowers to the necklace, place the center of each flower over the necklace wires.

Wrap wires around the group of necklace wires.

Coil the ends of the flower wires until secure.

Finish: Add a clasp to each end of the necklace.

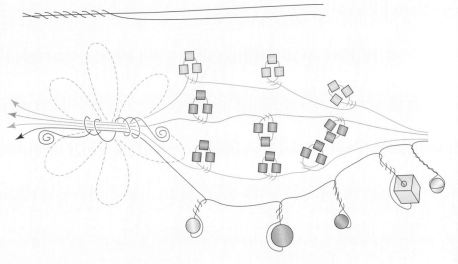

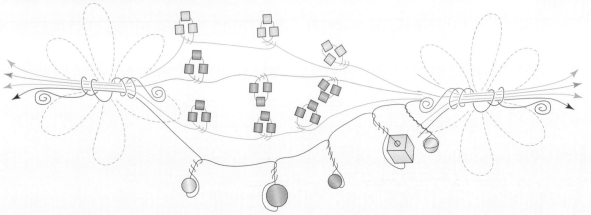

Fabulous Flowers Necklace

Every color of the rainbow may be found in this whimsical creation, making it the must-have accessory for your wardrobe.

Everyone will want to know where they can get one. Won't you be pleased to tell them that this design is a one-of-a-kind!

How to Make Necklace:

1. Begin with 2 wires, each 48" long. Twist them together about 12" from one end.

2. Begin working on the short 12" end.
   Add one Light Green crystal bead. Twist wires about 5 times to secure the bead.
   Repeat until you have 2 Light Green beads.
3. Now work on the longer end.
   Add one Light Green crystal (or dagger) bead. Twist the wire to secure the bead on a stem.
   Twist wires together about 5 times.
   Add one Light Green crystal bead. Twist wires about 5 times to secure the bead.
4. FLOWER BUD: Add Bud 1 (follow the diagram to add a Green crystal with a seed bead on the end, then add two seed bead buds) twisting each section securely as you go.
5. Continue by adding a crystal, a crystal (or dagger) bead on a stem, a crystal, another FLOWER BUD, a crystal (or dagger) bead on a stem, and a crystal.
6. Thread 21 Light Green seed beads on one wire. Twist wire stem to form a leaf with a short stem. Repeat.

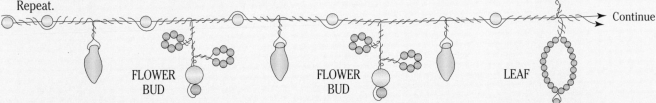

FLOWER BUD   FLOWER BUD   LEAF   Continue

7. Add another FLOWER BUD, a crystal and a crystal (or dagger) on a short stem.
8. Add a CENTER FLOWER BUD, a crystal and a crystal (or dagger) on a short stem.
   Repeat until you have 3 CENTER FLOWER BUDS.
9. Repeat "vine pattern" on the other side of the center flower buds. Continue adding beads to make the necklace design symmetrical.
   Add a clasp to each end of the necklace.

Continue Beading

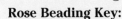

CENTER FLOWER BUD

How to Make a Rose:

10. Cut a 1/2" octagon (6 holes x 6 holes) from 14 count plastic canvas.
11. Thread 5 White beads onto a 12" length of wire. Working up and down on the canvas, attach beads near the center of canvas. Repeat until you have 3 strips near the center.
12. Thread 7 beads onto the wire. Attach beads on the outer rows of the canvas interlocking the rows. Repeat until you have 7 strips.
13. Thread a Lavender crystal in the center.
    Twist wires on the back of canvas. Flatten wires and cut off excess wire.

Rose Beading Key:
1 through 3 have 5 beads. All others have 7 beads.

1. ————————   6. ————————
2. ————————   7. ————————
3. ————————   8. ————————
4. ————————   9. ————————
5. ————————   10. ————————

Add Roses to Necklace:

14. Cut 5 leather 1/2" circles, or use metal circles.
    Sandwich necklace wires between the rose and circle. Glue rose to base and circle with E6000.

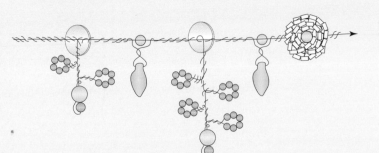

SUPPLIERS - Most craft and variety stores carry an excellent assortment of supplies. If you need something special, ask your local store to contact the following companies:

Artistic Wire, 630-530-7567, Elmhurst, IL
Beadalon, 800-824-9473, W. Chester, PA
Darice, 800-321-1494, Strongsville, OH
Helby Imports, 732-969-5300, Carteret, NJ

MANY THANKS to my friends for their cheerful help and wonderful ideas!
Kathy McMillan • Jennifer Laughlin
Janie Ray • Donna Kinsey
Patty Williams • Marti Wyble